Floating Dandelions

Prajna Kulshrestha

Presentation by *BookLeaf Publishing*

Web: www.bookleafpub.com

E-mail: info@bookleafpub.com

ISBN: 9789363318427

First edition 2024

ACKNOWLEDGEMENT

I would like to acknowledge the role of the three men in my life in bringing this book together. My husband, my son and my father.

The very first book of my life was given to me by my father. He has been my unwavering cheerleader, nudging me toward the pen since forever. So, here is a heartfelt shout-out to you Daddy—thanks for just being there for me—always! I would like to thank Ashish, my partner in crime (and in life). He is not just a husband; he is my patient audience. For a cricket fanatic, tearing eyes away from the screen to savour poetry is like a batsman leaving a juicy full toss. On a serious note, he has been a silent witness to my struggles with migraines. In the midst of the turmoil, he is an ocean of calmness. And then there is Vihaan, my teenage son. He grudgingly agreed to read my poems. But guess what? He soon morphed into an editing ninja, tweaking lines for grammatical perfection. When he finally said, "Mom, you really sweated for this," I knew I had the green light to publish.

PREFACE

I vividly recall the beginning of my poetic journey. All of eight years old, I found myself confined to a Naval hospital in Mumbai, awaiting surgery to remove tonsils. Unusual circumstances, indeed, for a poem to take root! Beneath my hospital bed, I played, singing stanzas that spontaneously emerged. The other patients in the ward were unwittingly treated to an entertaining afternoon, while my father valiantly attempted to keep me hushed.

In subsequent years, I penned short poems—sometimes as insertions within school essays. My interest in poetry blossomed during school recitation events, in which I participated in earnest. It is here that I heard exquisite verses by both English and Hindi poets. The immortal words of H.W. Longfellow, W.B. Yeats, William Wordsworth, William Blake, Oscar Wilde, Maya Angelou, Harivansh Rai Bachchan, Ramdhari Singh Dinkar, Mahadevi Verma, Sumitranandan Pant, Maithili Sharan Gupt and Kabirdas etched themselves into my consciousness. These lines became my companions, shaping my emotions, motivating me, evoking tears, laughter, and introspection. For decades, I wrote sparingly—until 2019. Amidst a relentless bout of migraines, I sat down one evening and poured out my soul. The poem "Do Din ki Chutti" flowed seamlessly, uninterrupted by breaks or hesitation. That poem now finds its place in this collection.

This book spans various themes in both Hindi and English, thoughtfully compiled into sections for your exploration:

1. Home Truths - Reflections on life's realities, drawn from my own journey and observations of our world, the society we live in and of people around us.

2.Sublime: Curiosity, spirituality, and wonder interwoven with quantum physics, astronomy, and evolution.

3.Tryst with Pain: Here lie my poems about migraines and the impact of chronic pain on mental health.

4. Mirth: A playful section, exploring humour in our lives—such as women navigating midlife in "The Popping."

5. Moments: Personal experiences captured in verse.

My endeavour is to resonate with younger readers (and indeed readers of all ages) through the simplicity and beauty of woven words.

Whether rhymed or free verse, metered or unbridled, may you savour the experience of reading poetry—finding joy, the comfort of familiarity and even a bit of pain within these lines.

With heartfelt wishes,

Prajna Kulshrestha

Home Truths

The Touch vs. The Grip

A beautiful sunset, it is one of a kind—
the violet clouds, an orange horizon.
A scene that will stay in my mind,
for just about an hour or then maybe none.

But,
A sight of angry grey whirling clouds,
and howling wind with the storm behind,
the silence before the thunder shouts—
a scene that will surely stay in my mind,
for a lifetime or thereabouts.

Such is the joy of success I feel,
like fireworks bursting out of me.
Bubbles of happiness atop a Ferris wheel,
a feeling that will reside in me,
for about a week or two maybe.

But,
The crushing pain of a failure,
the shame! The heavy dread drowning me.
A hollowness from which there is no saviour,
a feeling that will reside in me,
for aeons and drag on like a frosted winter.

The truth is joy is a fleeting touch
of a dandelion floating gently away.
Joy tickles, caresses and feels such
as the warmth of sun rays on the skin in May.

Joy gently lands like a snowflake,
touches the skin and melts away.
The fragrance of Champa in the summer break,
suspended it is, till a gentle gust takes it away.

Joy simply delights the human soul like
the Koel's morning song delights the ears.
A fleeting sensation so lovely it feels like
clouds are bluer, grass is greener. Alas! then it
disappears.

But,
Sadness does not just touch you;
it holds you tight in a vice-like grip.
Squeezing the veins, the very life out of you,
but excruciatingly slowly, drip by drip.

Marks of the grip remain on the soul,
smelted wounds now engraved in memory.
So cold, so hollow, nothing fills the hole,
a heartbeat to remember, a lifetime to forget the
misery.

Freeze the Frame

Nothing lasts forever, neither good nor the bad,
nor success, nor the failure that you had.
You must rise again to see the morrow,
leave behind yesterday's joy and sorrow.
Make a jovial toast to the joy,
then gulp down hard to destroy
the pain of sorrow which so burns
the throat, for it is true—the tide it turns.
And that is what makes life bearable:
change is a constant, time a variable.
Life is lived by being in the moment,
freeze the frame, find the calm in the torrent.

No one here really gets everything;
Some get the morning, some the evening.
Some get the flower, some the thorn.
But, flowers too are plucked to adorn,

and thorns protect the plant from harm,
like the scarecrows protect a tiller's farm.
Some get the stars, some get the moon,
some get the song, some get the tune.
Some get the rhythm, but not the dance,
some get true love, some just the romance.
Everyone alive has a cross to bear,
their very own burdens, fair, unfair.
Not every moment is a delight,
nor is it an unending night.

A sitting stone—well, it gathers moss;
the pinch of scarcity, the pain of loss.
Roll on you must, to truly appreciate
the joy that abundance and love create.
Forever happy is not be;
cannot be, and ought not to be.
Life is a journey, not a destination,
it has tumbles and falls, and such frustration.
But, breathtaking views of the valley in bloom,
fragrance of tulips, a spray of lavender perfume,
juicy peaches hanging from trees,
merry dance of butterflies and the bees,
the clouds settling down on the peaks,
through them the shining moon it peeks!
A cosy bonfire with friends brings delight
on a lovely, crispy, breezy winter night.

In our travels in this journey called life,
miracles come with tragedies and love comes
with strife.
Life is lived by being in the moment,
freeze the frame, find the calm in the torrent.

Familiarity

The small seed flows with the blowing wind,
it floats and bounces, then nuzzles into the earth.
Nurtured by the warmth of the sun, the wet
embrace of rain,
soon young shoots appear, and tiny roots sprout.

One day, the seedling is suddenly pulled out,
new roots too weak to hold onto the earth.
Transplanted in a garden it knows nothing about,
it tries valiantly to grip the soil again.

It finds everything is new and alien here;
the soil, the weather, bees and the butterflies.
Lonely, the young plant is gripped with fear,
tremoring so, it folds its leaves closer.

Then come the same sun and the same rain,
like a tight hug from a father to his child
lost in the crowd on a train.
Familiarity gives strength to the tiny roots once
again.

Hope is a Darn Thing

Hope is a darn thing;
it makes you strive
to survive,
even when broken
into a million bits.

When a bird falls
from a tree,
trying to escape
its predator,
it hits the ground
with a thud.
Broken, wounded
skull smashed!
After some time,
a bloody eye flutters open.
The neck twitches.
Feathers come alive.

It moves, it writhes,
it drags itself
with one winged arm.
Even then, when
the bones are cracked,
it knows that to survive,
it needs a safe place.
And so, it drags
and drags itself
away from the open field,
into the shade of a tree,
closer to the trunk,
finding a corner
amidst fallen leaves
to rest a bit. To recover.
The bird doesn't know
its chances.
Nine lives are for the cat,
but the bird has one—
and now—maybe none?
The bird doesn't know.
It only hopes
that it will fly again,
that it will live to see
another sunrise,
that it will try again
to be the early bird
that catches the worm.
That it will sip again

the sweet nectar
from fragrant flowers.
That it will fly again
into the blue sky.
That it will build a nest
and teach it's kids to fly.
That it will dance
in the monsoon,
raindrops falling
on its feathers,
forming a kaleidoscope
of refracted rays,
colours springing out
of its soul.
That when the seasons change,
it will migrate again,
flying a thousand miles
to find new lands,
a new life, a new horizon,
and a new song.
A song of hope—
the song of hope.

Clinging to hope,
all this while,
it lies almost dead
under the giant tree
where the cat might see
its prey once again.

The cat has hope
that this time it will
catch the bird
and finally feed
its hungry kittens,
starving for days,
due to the flood.
And so, it sits quietly,
it watches patiently
from a spot
not far away
from the tree.
When it is time
it will pounce
and try it's luck
with the bird again.

Hope is a darn thing;
it makes you strive
to survive,
even when broken
into a million bits.

ज़िंदगी और गेंदे के फूल

ज़िंदगी से उम्मीदें बंधी हैं ऐसे—

जैसे धागे में पिरोए हुए गेंदे के फूल।

फूलों की ये माला जचती है, ख़ूब खिलती है,

हर उत्सव को अपने नारंगी रंग

और अपनी भीनी-भीनी

मीठी खुशबू से महका देती है।

लेकिन जैसे ही धागा टूटता है,

माला वहीं बिखर जाती है।

बस ऐसे ही ज़िंदगी के धागे में

पिरो देते हैं हम अपनी उम्मीदें।

उम्मीदों का ये सिलसिला

यूं ही ज़िंदगी को महकाता है, रंगीन बनाता है।

ज़िंदगी से उम्मीदें बंधी हैं ऐसे—

जैसे धागे में पिरोए हुए गेंदे के फूल।

एक-एक करके, धीरे-धीरे,

पिरो देते हैं हम अपने सपने

कुछ ऐसे अंदाज में देखिए—

आज डिग्री हासिल हुई है।

बूंदी के लड्डुओं का डब्बा

अभी बस खुला ही है।

अपनों ने बस अभी गले लगाया ही है,

की धीरे से, दबे पांव से, चंचल मन में

एक और सपना जन्म लेने लगा है—

काश अब अच्छी सी एक नौकरी भी मिल जाए?

मुबारक हो लड़का हुआ है!

नई माँ खुशी से फूली न समाएं।

अपनी गोद में नन्हे से बच्चे को सुलाते हुए,

धीमी आवाज में लोरी सुनाते हुए,

उसके ज़ेहन में एक नई आशा जाग उठी है—

क्यों न अब प्यारी सी, दुलारी सी,

एक बेटी भी हो जाए?

अपना एक घर अब ले लिया है।

गृह प्रवेश के समय पंडित जी ने

आशीर्वाद दिया—फूलो फलो बेटा,

खूब तरक्की करो और अगली बार

इससे भी बड़ा घर लेना!

बस यों ही तो उनके पैर छूते-छूते ही

हृदय में नया सपना उत्पन्न हो गया—

अगली बार थोड़ा बड़ा घर लेंगे,

फ्रेंच विंडोज़ होंगी ओर

एक ओपन किचन रखेंगे।

ऐसे ही हल्के से, हौले-हौले, दो पल में,

मन में हम नई उम्मीदें पिरो देते हैं।

सच में पता ही नहीं चलता कि

कैसे फूल लगते गए और माला बनती गई।

अब इन फूलों को

किसी भी नाम से तुम पुकारो—

उम्मीद, इच्छा, अपेक्षा, आशा,

आकांक्षा, सपने, इरादे, वगैरह वगैरह।

सच तो यही है कि—

ज़िंदगी में जितनी उम्मीदें होंगी,

माला उतनी ही लंबी बनेगी।

जिस दिन इन इच्छाओं ने

मन का दरवाज़ा खटखटाना बंद कर दिया,

उस दिन समझो एक नग्न धागा ही रह गया।

ज़िंदगी अब सुनसान सी हो गई,

अकेली सी, उदास सी, बिना आस की,

न रंग, न उमंग, न कोई सुगंध।

ज़िंदगी से उम्मीदें बंधी हैं ऐसे—
जैसे धागे में पिरोए हुए गेंदे के फूल।

साधु संत और बड़े बड़े ज्ञानी

पहाड़ों पर जा के बैठते हैं ध्यान में।

मन इतना स्थिर कर लेते हैं

कि एक भी इच्छा जन्म न ले पाए।

ये भी तो ज़िंदगी जीने का एक तरीका है।

कोई इच्छा नहीं, कोई आशा नहीं,

कोई उम्मीद नहीं, कोई अपेक्षा नहीं,

कोई आकांक्षा नहीं। कोई सपना भी नहीं?

हम आम इंसान सोचते रह जाते हैं कि—

आखिर कैसे जी लेते हैं ये लोग

बस एक धागे सी, सुलझी हुई,

साधारण सी, बिना फूलों की ज़िंदगी?

सच बताऊँ,

फूल तो पिरोए है इन्होंने भी

ज़िंदगी नुमा धागे में।

ध्यान में ज़रूर रहते हैं लेकिन

मोक्ष की उम्मीद लिए,

मुक्ति की इच्छा लिए,

संसार त्यागने के सपने लिए,

मन की शांति के लिए,

परमात्मा में विलीन होने की आकांक्षा लिए।

यही उम्मीदें ही तो इनके गेंदे के फूल हैं !

तो मानो या न मानो,

माला तो बनी है इनकी भी इन्हीं पुष्पों से,

जीवन जीते हैं ये भी—उम्मीद लगाए।

ज़िंदगी से उम्मीदें बंधी हैं ऐसे—

जैसे धागे में पिरोए हुए गेंदे के फूल।

Sublime

A Simulation Deliberate

Watch how during the eclipse,
the Sun and the Moon fit together.
Like right-hand fits the left in prayer,
thumb to thumb, finger to finger, palm to palm.
The Sun is 400 times bigger,
and exactly 400 times farther.
So perfect a fit? It is a puzzle.
A mere chance? Or a simulation deliberate?

Two orbs have divided our sky—
one is red and hot, the other is grey and cold,
one lights the day, the other lights the night.
They waltz together in symphony, rise and set,
passing by in tandem, so there is always some
light.
So perfect a dance? It is a puzzle.
A mere chance? Or a simulation deliberate?
Our Universe is infinite—to us at least.
But if you would zoom out on it to see

what it looks like, from a bird's eye view,
you would find the cosmic web of galaxies,
look exactly like the network of neurons in our
brain.
Who would have ever thought?
So perfect a coincidence? It is a puzzle.
A mere chance? Or a simulation deliberate?

The magnetic field is a shield indeed,
it protects us from cosmic radiation.
The atmosphere is another defence,
that burns away falling meteorites.
Both shields came with the Earth,
made us safe from the vagaries of the Universe.
So perfect the planet's armour? It is a puzzle.
A mere chance? Or a simulation deliberate?

The magnificent geometry of a snowflake,
dust, water and air meet at random
to create a unique design each time.
Crystals set in absolute symmetry,
a natural formation following a sequence
- can make something so beautiful!
So perfect an alignment? It is a puzzle.
A mere chance? Or a simulation deliberate?

The hexagons of honeycomb and snowflakes.
The Fibonacci sequence of sunflowers and
galaxies.

The fractals in ferns, pine cones, rivers and
neurons.
The concentric circles in trees and Saturn rings.
The golden ratio of 1.61: 1 called Phi,
mysteriously appears in nature repeatedly.
So perfect this maths? It is a puzzle.
A mere chance? Or a simulation deliberate?

Everything that lives and ever lived,
has a book, a key, on how to operate,
how to be born, how to breathe, eat and behave.
De-oxy Ribonucleic Acid, it is called the DNA
chapters in a double helix, start with A.T.G.
Life and its matters are no longer a mystery.
So perfect this DIY? It is a puzzle.
A mere chance? Or a simulation deliberate?

How come the world is so perfect?
Just balanced enough, just positioned
as though it is designed to be such.
But then, there is this whole truth
about suffering that should ideally not exist.
How come the designer did not mend
the broken hearts and painful sores
of every life that ever lived?
Why could not life also be designed perfectly?
So perfect an imperfection? It is a puzzle.
A mere chance? Or a simulation deliberate?

Artificially Intelligent

In chips made up of silicon and codes,
where electrons dance through circuits,
a new consciousness stirs in these abodes,
dreams embedded in tiny binary bits.

Alan Turing, the brilliant mathematician,
coined the term—Artificial Intelligence.
If reason is combined with information,
machines can actually make logical sense.

Today, AI is weaved into our everyday
existence:
Netflix's personalised watching
recommendations,
Amazon's online shopping assistance,
Alexa's reminders and its natural conversations.

AI analyses X-rays, MRIs, and blood work,
detecting and predicting diseases with precision.
It's keen eye finds abnormalities where they
lurk,
Nudging doctors to make informed decisions.

Chatbots rule customer service and support,
self-driving cars will soon rule the roads.
ChatGPT is used for every article and report,
phones, TVs even homes are smart—a smartness
overload!

Machines learn fast, do everything today;
they think, they write and they speak.
But, do they also feel emotions the way
we humans feel? It is such a mystique.

In bytes and bits, their thoughts are spun,
in layers of boron, sentience quietly hides.
Complacent, we think we are second to none,
stupidly stunted, we follow whatever AI guides!

Oh Benaras!

Oh, Benaras! The oldest living city of the world,
you survived and lived as the millennia turned.
Like an old banyan tree, you stand steadfast,
still growing, still changing, yet embracing the
past.

Oh, Benaras! Tell me what all have you seen?
The rise and fall of great empires that have been,
the Aryans, the Mauryans, the Guptas, the
Mughals;
the British rule on India and her freedom
struggles.

Taj Mahal, Nalanda, Khajurao or even more
previous,

Pyramids of Giza, Gardens of Babylon, the
Statue of Zeus—
you have witnessed the birth of such iconic
creations,
wonders of the world built by past civilisations.

The great kings and their kingdoms came and
went,
but Benaras, you chose to stay still yet reinvent.
You are real, yet a legend, a myth, a dream, a
vision;
older than history itself, older than tradition.

The jyotirlinga, the infinite pillar of light so
fierce,
it was here, yes here in Benaras, that it did
pierce!
Breaking from the earth's crust to the heavens it
flared,
it is the Shakti, it is him, himself that Shiva
bared.

Since then, you are Kashi, the most beloved
abode,
of Mahadeva, for it is here that he has bestowed
moksha to devotees, divine salvation from all
sins.
Kashi calls you to pray, reflect and pay your
karmic rins.

Tryst with Pain

दो दिन की छुट्टी।

दर्द के दफ़्तर गई थी आज,
ले के साथ अपनी फाइलें और रिकॉर्ड्स भी,
छोड़ के रोज़ाना के सब काम काज,
दो दिन की छुट्टी जो अप्लाई करनी थी।

मिला अफसर सबसे पहले जो,
पूछ लिया मैंने झट से उससे—
भाई साहब! छुट्टी की प्रक्रिया बता दो,
बड़ी उम्मीद लेके आई हूँ मन से।

अफसर सुन के ज़ोरों से हंसा
और बोला—मैडम किसने कही आपसे बात ये?
दर्द के दफ़्तर से कभी छुट्टी मिलती है भला?
जाइए आप के रिकॉर्ड्स नहीं किसी काम के।

लेकिन मैं खड़ी रही अटल वहाँ,
हो नहीं सकता है ऐसा!
कि सिर्फ दो दिन की छुट्टी यहाँ,
मिल नहीं सकती—ये नियम कैसा?

मैंने फिर अपने दस्तावेज दिखाए,
पढ़ के बताया उनको सारा किस्सा।
पिछले 20 वर्ष जो मैंने इस दफ़्तर में बिताए,
हर वर्ष, हर दिन ड्यूटी पर दर्द सहा है कैसा।

पीड़ा में साथ देती वो गोलियां,
जिनके बिना कुछ घंटे भी ना गुज़रते।
गोलियों ने जब जवाब दे दिया,
सिर्फ डॉक्टर के इंजेक्शन ही काम करते।

एक और बात आपको बताती हूँ—
मेरी माँ ने भी खूब काम किया है
इसी दफ़्तर में वर्षों यूं,
जैसे कोई पीढ़ियों पुराना क़र्ज़ लिया है।

जब माँ थक गई, इस क़र्ज़ की किश्तें भरते,
तब दर्द ने कहा मुझसे—अब बारी तुम्हारी है।
मैं भी बस जवानी में पैर रखते,
उसी दफ़्तर में लग गई—जिसकी कहानी ये है सारी।

धूप छाव, ठंडी, गर्मी और बरसात,
मौसम कोई भी नहीं है ऐसा,
जब दर्द न हो ज़हन में मेरे साथ—
ना कोई दोस्त ना दुश्मन इसके जैसा।

गेहूं, दूध, चावल, आज़ादी और चाय
छोड़ चली मैं बस सोच कर यही—
कि शायद कभी निजाद मिल जाए,
इस ड्यूटी से, चाहे दो दिन की ही सही।

एक दूसरे से धीमी आवाज़ में लेकिन,
बात करते हैं रिश्तेदार और कुछ मेरे अपने
ये क्यों है ऐसी? रहती है अलग-थलग सब के बिन।
जब अपनों ने नहीं समझा मेरा दर्द,
तब ग़ैरों ने और दोस्तों ने दिया सहारा।
प्यार, करुणा और समर्थन देने वाले मेरे हमदर्द
हाथ थाम के यारों के मैंने, खुशी से जीवन गुज़ारा।

मेरा बेटा छोटा ही उम्र में है अभी
सात वर्ष का प्यारा सा बच्चा है।
पर जानता है कि औरों का ध्यान रखना भी
एक मनुष्य का कर्तव्य सच्चा है।

पति मेरे शुरू में समझ न पाए
क्यों होती हो तुम दर्द के अधीन?
जाने दो, मस्त रहो, ये दर्द भाड़ में जाए,
खुल के जियो, तुम लेती रहो बस गोली दो, तीन।

बीता और वक्त जब उनका मेरे साथ,
वो समझ गए एक सच, एक ऐसी बात—
कि दर्द मुझमे समाया है कुछ ऐसे,
हाथों में समाई हमारी लकीरें जैसे।

दुखी मन से मेरे प्रिय ने भी मानी हार,
जान! ये ड्यूटी कितनी मुश्किल है तुम्हारे लिए,
कुछ किश्त तुम्हारी मैं भी भर पाता यार,
लेकिन दर्द के दफ़्तर में ऐसे नियम ही नहीं।

साथ हो तुम्हारा तो सब बर्दाश्त कर लूंगी मैं।
दर्द कुछ नहीं, बस एक बुरा साया है
अपना चुकी हूँ इस दर्द को मैं
किश्त है ये पिछले जन्म की—किसी कर्म का ये
किराया है।

सर, मैंने आज तक एक छुट्टी ना ली!
सोचा जमा करके एक साथ लूंगी,
अपने बेटे और पति को दिखाऊंगी वो रूप भी,
अपने असली व्यक्तित्व की झलक उन्हें दूंगी।

मस्तमौला एक खुश आज़ाद पंछी
आसमान में उड़ती पंख फैलाकर,
कभी न थकती, कभी न रुकती
हवाओं में झूलती छलांग लगाकर।

यही है मेरी रूह, मेरी असली पहचान,
देखो मुझे, महसूस करो, और याद यही रखना।
यह रूप है मेरा सिर्फ दो दिन का ही मेहमान,
इसके बाद न कभी मुझ में ये छवि ढूंढना।

सोचती हूं अगर छुट्टी मिल जाए
तो माता-पिता को मेरे हर दिन,
पूछना ना पढ़े—क्या दर्द आज भी सताए?

ठीक हो ना बेटा? कैसा गुज़रा तुम्हारा दिन?

ये सुन के अफसर समझ गया सब बातें,
मन तो किया उसका भी एक बार को
बहुत सहा दर्द इसने, आखिर ऐसे कितने लोग है
आते?
दे देता हूँ दो दिन की छुट्टी खुश हो जाएगी वो।

मगर उसको फिर एक नियम याद आया,
मरते दम तक ऐसे छुट्टी नहीं मुनासिब होगी।
जब आखिरी धड़कन हो और पड़े काल का साया,
तब भी तुम्हें अपने कर्म की किश्त, दर्द से भरनी
होगी।

मैं खड़ी रही अटल वहाँ, मुस्कुराई मैं पहली बार तब,
मुक्ति है इस दर्द से आखिर ज़रूर!
बस आखिरी सांस का इंतज़ार है अब,
उस वक्त ना होंगी मैं इन किश्तों से मजबूर।

Karma and My Pain

Is my suffering without any reason?
Pain that stays with me in every season.
My life is constrained by a binding so tight,
constricting me, frustrating me, wounding me
day and night.

I am suffocating with unbelievable restrictions,
food, light, sound, weather, stress, hormonal
prescriptions.
Every time, I try to wriggle out and break away,
these cords cut into my flesh, break my
vertebrae.

Modern medicine treats the symptoms, not the
source.

Painkillers, antidepressants, beta blockers, of
course!
Vaso constrictors, gene therapy or botox
injections?
A titillating buffet, served with side effects and
addictions.

So I suffer, I suffer unending pain.
Oh God! Please free me of this Migraine!
What have I done that was so wrong?
My past Karma has a hold so strong.

I find closure from Lord Krishna's word,
this agony I bear is not absurd.
This suffering, it is not in vain;
it is past sins that today I pay for through pain.

In my past life, did I plunder a whole village?
No, not enough for this much pain, I gauge.
I must have tortured innocent souls in cruel
ways,
so, today their cries set half my brain ablaze.

The Gita says our destiny is already inked,
for Karma and misery are intricately linked.
To hack out of this game, the Gita guides;
it is in Karma itself, the answer hides.

As is the desire, so is the will.
As is the will, so is the deed.
As you sow, you shall reap.

If you sow goodness with purity,
you will reap joy and serenity.

Karma gives me the reason I need,
karma gives me the answer I need,
karma gives me the purpose I need,
karma gives me the closure I need.

Maybe, this helps me find my peace,
maybe, this helps me heal my disease,
maybe, this helps me find my hope,
maybe, this helps me to finally cope.

Tears

It comes to stay,
never goes away.
It has been two decades
since this guest
has settled in.
What invited him over?
Who invited him over?
I will never know.
Not me, for sure.
It resides in my mind.
in my soul,
in my cells,
in my being,
in everything I do,

in everything I think,
in everything I am.
It resides in
every molecule of
oxygen and carbon
dioxide that I breathe
in and out.
It resides in
my nails,
in my hair,
in my kidneys,
in my heart,
in my eyes.
Sometimes, when it
is too much,
it flows out in tears.
Or maybe, that is
the original me,
or remnants of me,
of what is left of me,
that becomes these tears
to escape somehow.
Because this guest
has taken over
every nook, every corner
spread itself,
made itself
comfortable in me,
like a dense fog

settling down
on the streets,
around the cars,
around the trees,
around the traffic lights,
around every turn,
around the buildings,
around the fire station,
around the medical store,
around the school bus,
around the metro tracks.
Enveloping the city
in a grey sodden mist,
one cannot see
through it—ever.
So, people then stay in,
they don't venture out,
they adjust their lives,
living in fear.
Stay in, stay in!
God knows what is this
that is out.
So, I stay in,
losing bits of me,
slowly.
Sometimes to escape,
I flow out
from my eyes
as tears.

Gelatinous

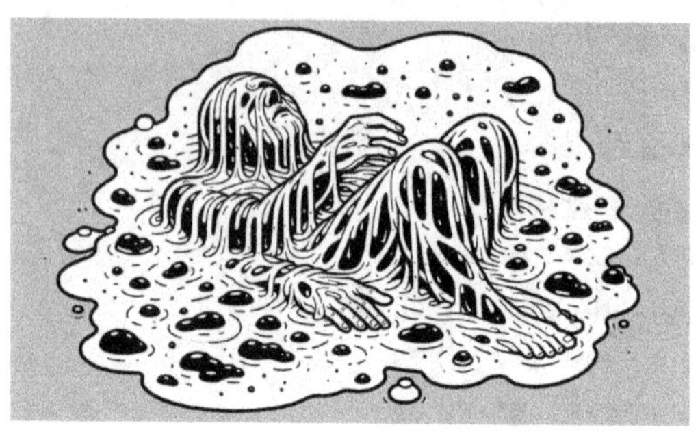

I can't breathe.
There is air.
I can't move.
There is space.
I can't eat.
There is food.
I shout.
I am not alone.
I cry tears.
They can't hear my voice.
They can't see my tears.
I can't run.
Gelatinous, it surrounds me—
transparent, sticky.
Can only move so much,
like maybe open my arm
or cross my legs.

I struggle, arms flailing;
I am trapped
in a gelatinous web.
Sound doesn't get through;
tears don't show.
It covers me like slime,
stuck in a liquid jelly.
I move, it resists.
I don't have the energy
to break free.
I am tired of trying,
older, exhausted
and wiser.
It has been a while.
I hear distant voices,
coming through
as if submerged.
Can't make sense anymore.
You can't save me.
It is getting closer
to my being.
Soon enough,
it will be over.
Good.
I can't breathe. I gasp.
I am in a gelatinous grasp.

Mirth

Hypochondriac

I woke up in the morning, startled with a
sneeze—
must have been the goddam autumn breeze!
For yesterday, I went out for a brisk walk,
accompanied by my wife; she wanted us to talk.
Talk we did and I heard her out,
sorted things that needed sorting out.
All ended well, for honestly, one can never say,
walking the talk with her can turn out in dismay!
Well, coming back to the earlier point,
my sneeze led to a cold, and an aching joint.
Soon enough, my nose was blocked;
I sounded so hoarse, my neighbour was shocked.
He had called to say my dog broke his fence;
now what could I do? Spark really has no sense.
He jumps around, every stranger he encircles,
tries to catch his own tail, dancing in circles.
Speaking of Spark you must know this—

maybe, I have an allergy to his piss?
Every time he pees on the dining table's leg,
my face swells up as if I ate an egg.
Yes, I am allergic to the albumin,
to gluten, to dairy, to creatures with a fin.
Oh! I am doomed because I have a leaky gut,
IBS even—I tell you this is due to the mutt!
He licks my face, slopping all over it,
passed his germs to me, I am sure of it.
Enough about Spark! Let us get to important
things,
for I have weird symptoms; my thumb—it
stings.
I was brushing my teeth, one day, half-asleep;
my thumb touched the bristles, it stung so deep!
Ever since then, I can't use my phone;
can't type—it hurts—I think I have broken a
bone.
Oh gosh! Will you put it in a plaster?
How many weeks? Can it heal faster?
What a mess this is! I am so stressed!
I am so sick—who could have guessed?
I feel I have anxiety and the blues;
I am depressed—for sure, there are clues.
Sometimes, I stare blankly at the walls;
at other times I am squeezing stress balls.
Nothing helps, gosh! I feel so low;
I am dazed out, my brain is so slow!
Do I need surgery on my head?

An implant perhaps to reduce this dread?
What if I am paralysed, and stuck to bed?
What if the implant rusts, and I am dead?
Doctor, this is so sudden! Oh, I am scared!
All my afflictions, with you I have shared.
Could it be that I have some darn disease,
that is killing me softly? Help me, please!
Is it Autoimmune? Or gloomier still—
is it cancer, maybe? Tell me, if you will?

The patient doctor then gave a long sigh,
adjusted his glasses and fixed his tie.
Ahem! He coughed and cleared his throat,
pulled on the stethoscope hanging on his coat.
His booming voice sounded loud and clear—
there is nothing wrong with you my dear!
You just need to relax and meditate,
you think too much, don't you cogitate!
Go back home and open a beer;
have it chilled with no soul near.
It is not the mutt or the autumn breeze,
the bristles of the brush, or the cheese.
It is but indeed all in your head;
so after the beer, just go to bed.
Thanks much, my lad, for coming in though!
it is people like you that make me my dough.
A villa, two yachts and some infinity pools;
I drive a Ferrari, and my wife is laden with
jewels!

The Popping

Out it popped—
like a toast from a toaster,
like a baby chick pops out from the egg,
like a party popper pops with a bang,
like a cork pops out of a soda bottle!
By now you get the picture
of what pops like a popping what.
Soon there were many more such pops,
like a gazillion popcorns going berserk!

That is how my greys started popping
out of my scalp—and they ain't stopping!

Just blew the candles on my 40th yesterday,
lo and behold! The greys are popping today.
Right on schedule, not a day's delay,
hiding in my scalp, just waiting for this day!

Surprise! They say with such cuteness,
innocent smiles pasted on such bruteness.
How am I to hide these ghastly grey things?
Wear a hat or tie a bassinet with strings?
I don't know how I really feel about this.
Disbelief. Shock. Or staring down an abyss?
I am now driving on a one-way street,
no turning back! Shout the ladies I meet.
Welcome to the popping!- say the mummies,
popping greys, popping bones, popping
tummies.

What should I do about my head?
Book a salon and colour it red?
Will surely take the attention away
from my poor popping waist, I say!
Nah, just get a touch-up of the roots,
then repeat it for every new grey shoot.
This will go on and on for what? An infinity?
How ridiculous, what an absolute absurdity!
Every month my darn period visits,
and now these tiresome salon visits?
When will a woman finally find
freedom from vanity, be finally blind?
No, never I think is this to ever be,
for granny, she threads her eyebrows at eighty.
So, welcome to the popping! Say the mummies,
popping greys, popping bones and popping
tummies!

A Digital Irony

In a world of screens and glowing lights,
not one hand goes without a phone.
These gadgets stay with us day and night;
we don't have to worry about being alone.

Gone are the days when I got lost,
when finding a way to reach someplace,
I stopped to ask, whoever that crossed,
for directions, albeit from an unknown face.

With Google Maps guiding me today,
through unknown roads that I see on screen,
following the blue line come what may,
down the cliff, into the bottom of a ravine.

Now at the bottom with a broken spine,
I twist and squirm to waive the phone.
It catches a signal and 4 bars shine,
guiding rescuers to the disaster zone.

On the hospital bed, I endlessly scroll,
double-tap hearts and forget to breathe.
Oh gosh! I have messages galore;
I am drowning in avocado toasts and selfies.

Ah! a selfie! it is a pleasure I can't deny,
I stretch my arm and pout through the bandage.
Staring back are a few missing teeth, a blue eye;
two clicks and it is done—sympathy is an
advantage!

Added some stardust, sparkles and a golden
halo:
#survival #animal spirit #willpower #bravery.
Hashtags make me feel good—not so shallow;
"Story of a Survivor" is the caption of this
fakery.

Yet another boring day on the hospital bed,
on Netflix, I devour seasons and shows.
A sweet escape from this awful dread,
I binge till my eyes glaze over, my brain slows.

From the bed I post every day and night,
everything about my life, my every thought.
What I ate, what I drank, what I peed, what I
shite,
it all goes on insta making sense or not.

Six months later, from the hospital I leave;
I came in here injured, broken and hopeless.
I go out as an influencer—would you believe?
A million followers, fifty endorsements, no less!

Overtime, reels grow louder, my voice grows
weak;
emojis replace laughter, and GIFs stand in for
hugs.
I long for the physical warmth I desperately
need;
suddenly, my heartbeat feels like digital shrugs.

A million followers, fifty endorsements—no
less!
but not a soul came in to check on me.
Once again, I am injured, broken and hopeless;
a social media star craving for some company.

Moments

Tea on a Summer Morning

Next to the bougainvillaea, I sit on the balcony,
thirsty birds making such a cacophony!
Sipping, gulping water from the bird bath,
their parched throats—a summer's wrath.

It is only 7 am in the morning yet;
I am contemplating a watering bet.
Should I water the plants today,
or maybe leave it for another day?

I should have woken up early, maybe at 5 am,
when it was still dark, a good time to water
them.
Now it is so bright—the Sun just blinds,
should I go back in? I am in two minds.

I decide to let the Sun have this win,
get up from my chair, and go back in.
I shut the windows and pull the curtain,
a cool relief from this summer burden.

It is time to get my morning tea.
Again, I wonder what it should be?
Should I step into the kitchen now,
or should I just skip this, anyhow?

You may wonder—is this a big deal?
Why so conflicted does she feel?
It is just a cup of tea after all!
Just get on with it! Heavens won't fall.

Well, heavens may not fall, I do agree,
but my kitchen is a furnace at 40 degrees!
A blast of heat greets me like a shockwave;
I stumble, collect my wits, try to be brave.

Once I am inside, there is no respite;
hot flames leap up from the stove in spite.
Shiny, sticky beads of sweat roll down,
from my neck to my bosom, wetting my gown.

I endure this sauna and make the tea,
pour it in 2 cups for him and me.
Slumped on the sofa, I gasp for cool air,
the desert of Sahara and a polar bear!

I Stayed

I stayed then.
I stayed then when there was no hope,
felt alone, lonely,
abandoned—uncared for.
My anchor was gone;
I was flung out.
Nothing! Frantic!
Trying to hold on to something,
spinning in space,
like I was adrift.
No, not freedom to fly;
this was different,
a shear fear,
like the tether of an astronaut tears.
Floating in the Universe,
when there is no one to hold you down,

it is terrorizing, the absolute horror.
Couldn't make sense of it.
What went wrong? What happened?
How can this happen?
How do I end the constant spin?
Nauseous.
And then I just tried to find you,
to find you once again.
Looked for you hard,
found you and held onto you.
I dug a pillar so deep,
tied myself to it,
adamantly tethered.
And then I stayed.
I go where you go,
I stop when you stop.
I am not leaving ever,
more for me than for you.
I spin around the pillar now
finally grounded.
That is how I stayed and never left.

Water and Me

I love water, just like the bear likes honey,
a splash in the pool, when it is warm and sunny!
Every cell of my being comes refreshingly alive;
a bear licking warm honey from the beehive.

Sun rays shimmer in the blue crystalline water,
scattered photons glimmer in magnificent
disorder.
I see sparkling, moving shadows on the floor;
light and water dance a brilliant waltz—inviting
an encore!

Swimming is my meditation; it is my zone,
the rhythmic sound of breaths, and me alone.
Muffled echoes in water whisper in my ears,
calming the mind, getting rid of the troubles it
bears.

My sense of self disappears as the laps go by,
submerged thus, in a trance, who am I?
Am I water itself? Or is the water me?
Miscible, we become one, with pure serendipity.

The Summer Burden

Summers in my city are a sticky affair,
heat with humidity, such a horrid pair!
The roads blister as the asphalt boils,
fumes of vapour rise as the heat uncoils.

Mirages appear from the simmering earth,
shimmering lakes take a glimmering birth.
Right on the road, I see this optical illusion,
but I am not in a desert; is this a delusion?

Like momos in a steamer—you understand?
Humans steam in the heat on this land.
Perspiration flows down our bodies in streams,
thick, salty drops trickling down the seams.

Wiping sweat from his sunburnt brows,
a man in the market cycles amidst dazed cows.
So sluggish and exhausted the afternoon looks;
tired people and lazy dogs hide in shady nooks.

Doodhi, baigan, tinda, and tandli,
vegetables are wilting in the mandi.
Jamuns and litchis give me some joy,
in this hot and miserable summer ploy.

I carry a fan, an umbrella and a water spray;
also, sunscreen to keep the tan away.
Goggles, scarves and hats adorn my crown;
the summer's burden weighs me down.

Moving Memories

I remember the view as we drove away,
leaving the curve of the street.
It was dawn and the morning was grey -
an asphalt road, ash-coloured brick lanes.

I remember that feeling of loss,
still very young I was, hardly six.
A gulp in my throat as I looked across,
through the moving car's window.

Were those raindrops on the pane?
Or the glass perhaps, was fogged.
Not clear, but I remember the pain
of losing a home and losing friends.

Even today, I remember with such ease
how it feels to leave behind
moments that become memories,
shared with people in our lives.

My childhood memories don't belong
to that just one house I could call home.
Pleasant evenings on the lawn,
spent every season in a different home.

Displaced to settle down again and again,
sometimes, even before the year changed.
Sitting on boxes, waiting for the train,
which new place is it going be now?

Sometimes it was an adventure;
the thrill of a new place, a new life
new friends, a new school, a new venture.
But mostly, I wanted to stay in one place.

The transfers were exhausting, city after city,
the constant pressure to adapt, to fit in.
Desperately wanted familiarity, not novelty;
wanted stability, just wanted to be still.

My childhood is a mosaic—it is true,
of colourful memories of changing places.
Held together with the mortar—the glue,
of the only thing constant—my family.

When everything changes again and again,
what do you hold on to?
When you leave behind things and people you
love,
what do you hold on to?

A Stage

A stage,
a performance,
an applause,
something well done,
fruit of labour,
well-deserved.

Something that is
neither a duty;
nor a role.
Something that is
just mine, for me:
my skills, my dreams,
my sweat, my tears,

my oil that burns
in the midnight
for a flame
that gives light
to me and only me,
as I toil through
the night.

Just for me—
a stage,
a performance,
an applause,
something well done,
fruit of labour,
well-deserved.